This book is designed for family participation during the Christmas season. You can adapt it's use to an existing nativity set or make your own from a pattern of your choice, either making the figures ahead or as you go through the book.
The "cue words" are underneath each picture of the nativity figures.
Say them aloud each time you pass each nativity figure to help you remember the meaning of Christmas.

If you begin this book on December 14th and do one page each day you will finish it on December 25th.

If you want to give yourself time for life's interruptions, start this activity book sometime the first week of December. You can also time things so that the last completed on the traditional arrival of the wisemen, January 6.

BLESSINGS!
Grandma

...doing simple things toge

For Christmas lessons and games go to
www.mygrandmatime.com
and type "Christmas" in the search bar.

"In the beginning God created the heavens and the earth." Genesis 1:1 (NIV)

The Bible tells us that God made us to be His friends.
When men disobeyed God's rules (Genesis 3) they were sinful
and could not be close to God.
God promised to send a Savior (Genesis 3:15)
so that we could be His friends again.
The empty manger reminds us of God's promise.

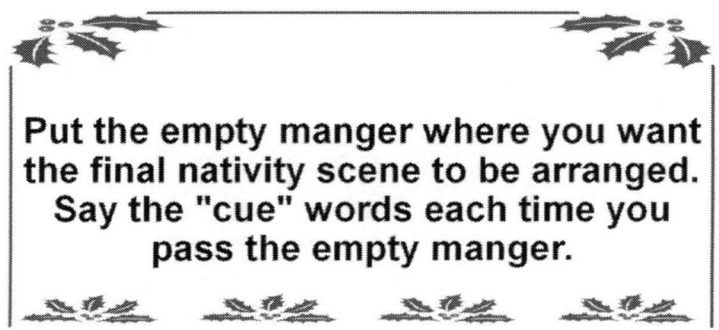

Put the empty manger where you want
the final nativity scene to be arranged.
Say the "cue" words each time you
pass the empty manger.

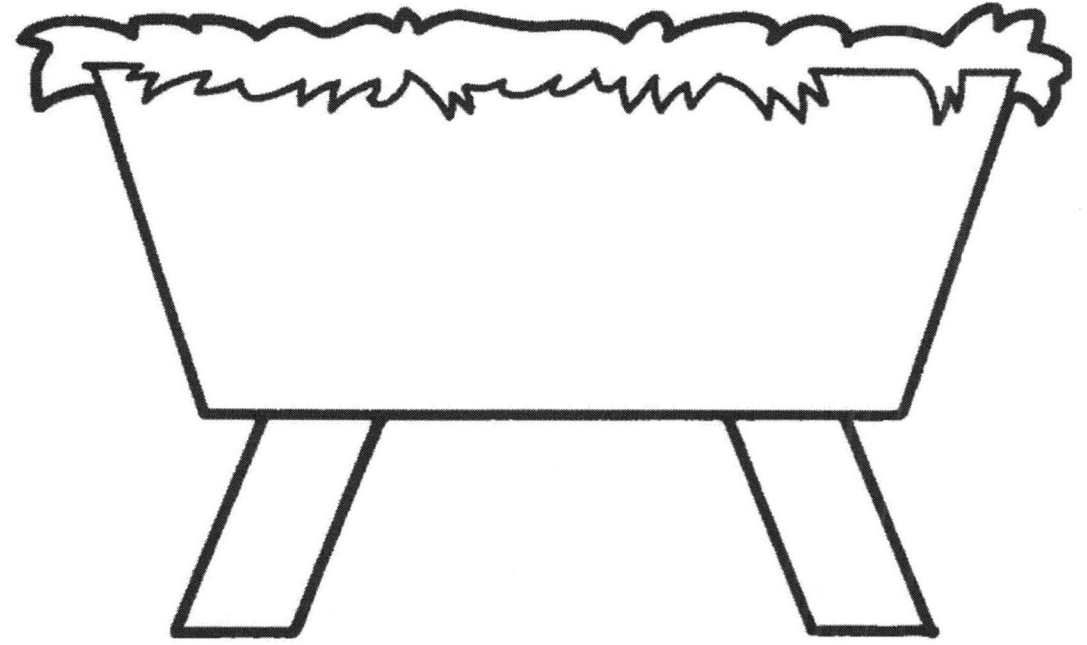

"Therefore the Lord Himself will give you a sign:
The virgin will be with child and will give birth to a son,
and will call Him Immanuel." Isaiah 7:14 (NIV)

From the time of creation to the time of Jesus' birth, God's prophets told about the coming Savior and asked people to be ready for Him. A star was sent to lead the wisemen to the manger before Jesus was born. The star reminds us to get ready for the Savior.

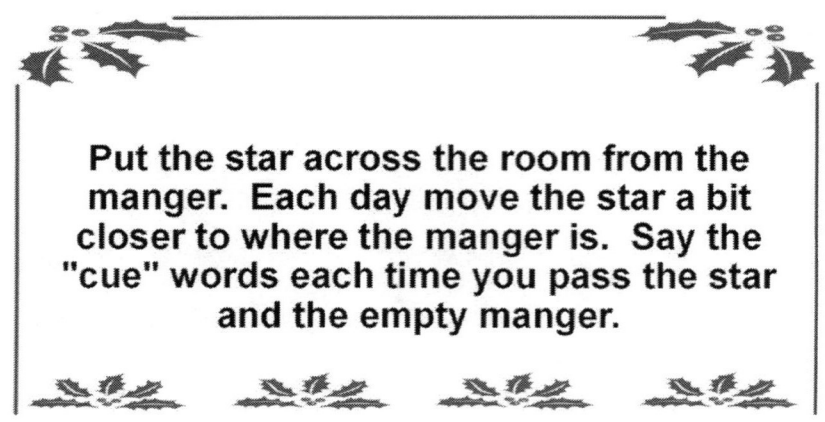

Put the star across the room from the manger. Each day move the star a bit closer to where the manger is. Say the "cue" words each time you pass the star and the empty manger.

"God sent the angel Gabriel to Nazareth, a town in Galilee, to a virgin pledged to be married to a man named Joseph, a descendant of David. The virgin's name was Mary." Luke 1:26-27 (NIV)

God's angels are His messengers.
God sent His angel to get things ready
for Baby Jesus to be born.

Put your angel in a high place over the manger. Move the star a bit closer to the manger. Say the "cue" words each time you pass the angel, the star, and the empty manger.

"I am the Lord's servant," Mary answered.
"May it be to me as you have said." Luke 1:38 (NIV)

Mary was happy to do what God wanted.
She even sang a song of joy. (Luke 2:46-55)
Mary reminds us to be willing servants.

Put Mary on your kitchen counter.
Move the star a bit closer to the manger.
Say the "cue" words each time you pass
Mary, the angel, the star,
and the empty manger.

A WILLING SERVANT

"Joseph son of David, do not be afraid to take Mary home as your wife, because what is conceived in her is from the Holy Spirit. She will give birth to a son, and you are to give Him the name Jesus, because He will save His people from their sins." Matthew 1:20-21 (NIV)

Joseph was happy to do what God wanted.
He took good care of both Mary and Jesus.

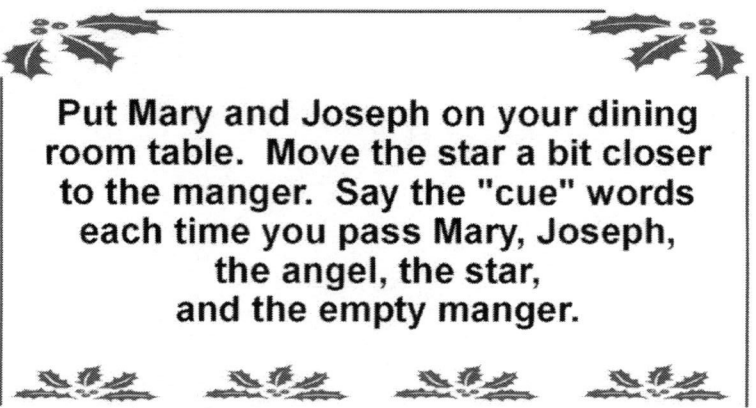

Put Mary and Joseph on your dining room table. Move the star a bit closer to the manger. Say the "cue" words each time you pass Mary, Joseph, the angel, the star, and the empty manger.

THE ADOPTING FATHER

"And she gave birth to her firstborn, a Son.
She wrapped Him in cloths and placed Him in a manger,
because there was no room for them in the inn." Luke 2:7 (NIV)

Many thought that the Savior would be born in a palace.
Jesus was born in a stable to show that He is both our Savior and our Friend.

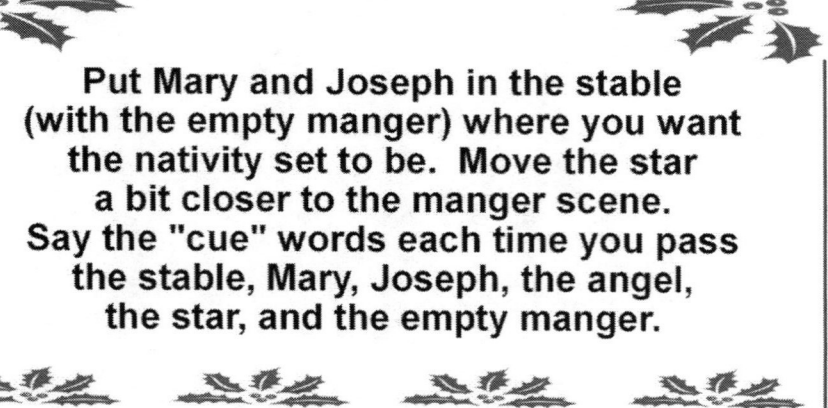

Put Mary and Joseph in the stable
(with the empty manger) where you want
the nativity set to be. Move the star
a bit closer to the manger scene.
Say the "cue" words each time you pass
the stable, Mary, Joseph, the angel,
the star, and the empty manger.

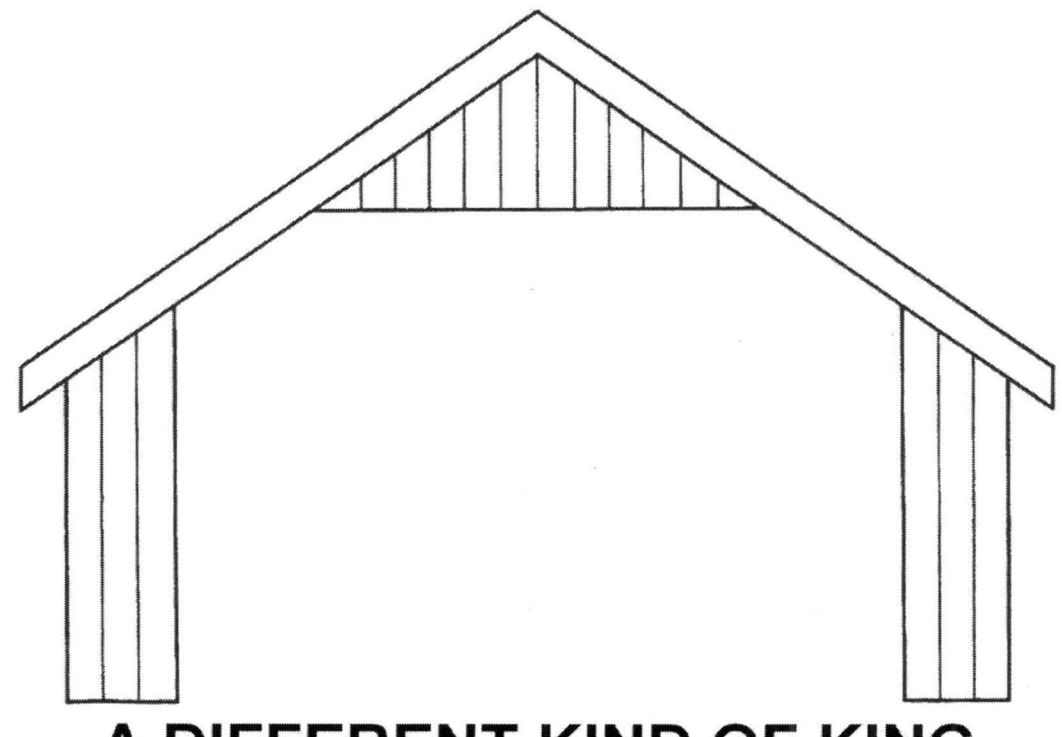

A DIFFERENT KIND OF KING

"For unto us a Child is born, unto us a Son is given,
and the government shall be upon His shoulder;
and His name shall be called Wonderful, Counselor,
the Mighty God, the Everlasting Father, the Prince of Peace." Isaiah 9:6

Can you think of a better gift than God's Son?
Jesus came to be our Friend and our Savior.

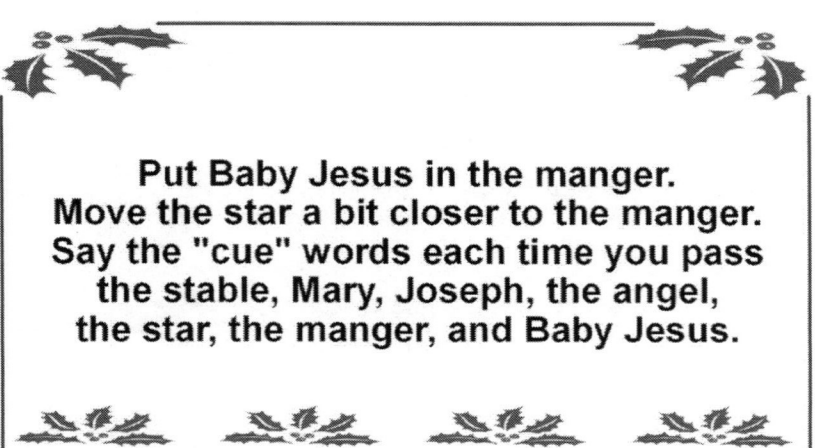

Put Baby Jesus in the manger.
Move the star a bit closer to the manger.
Say the "cue" words each time you pass
the stable, Mary, Joseph, the angel,
the star, the manger, and Baby Jesus.

THE BEST PRESENT OF ALL

"O Israel, put your hope in the Lord,
for with the Lord is unfailing love and with Him is full redemption.
He Himself will redeem Israel from all their sins." Psalm 130:7-8 (NIV)

The Bible says that Jesus is the Lamb of God.
Before Jesus, a lamb had to be sacrificed to pay for a man's sin.
Since Jesus came and died for us, He is our sacrifice for sin.

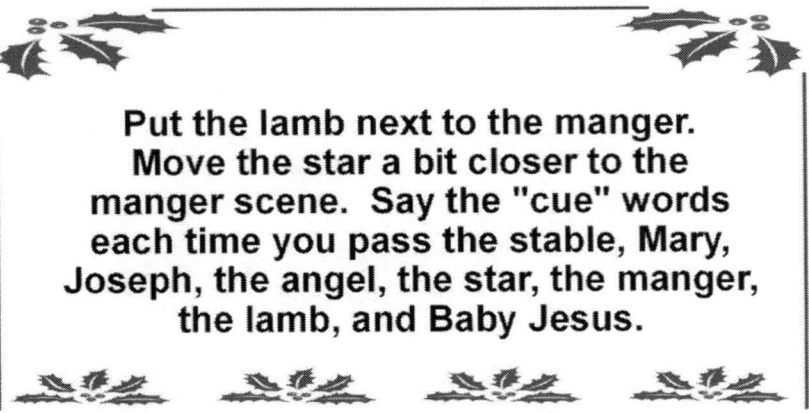

Put the lamb next to the manger. Move the star a bit closer to the manger scene. Say the "cue" words each time you pass the stable, Mary, Joseph, the angel, the star, the manger, the lamb, and Baby Jesus.

JESUS, THE LAMB OF GOD

"The shepherds returned, glorifying and praising God
for all the things they had heard and seen,
which were just as they had been told." Luke 2:20 (NIV)

The shepherds were told by the angels that Jesus was born.
After they had seen Jesus, they went and told others about what had happened.

Place the shepherd in the stable and shout it's "cue" words. Move the star a bit closer to the manger. Say the "cue" words each time you pass the stable, Mary, Joseph, the angel, the star, the manger, the lamb, the shepherd (SHOUT!), and Baby Jesus.

"Where is the One who has been born King of the Jews?
We saw His star in the east and have come to worship Him." Matthew 2:2 (NIV)

Just as the camels and wisemen searched for the new King,
we want to find Jesus and worship Him.

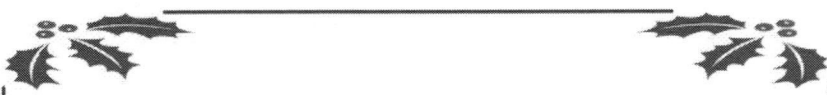

Place the camel under the star and
move them both a bit closer to the manger.
Repeat the "cue" words for the stable,
Mary, Joseph, the angel, the star,
the manger, the shepherd (shout!),
the camel, the lamb, and Baby Jesus.

"On coming to the house, they saw the child with His mother Mary, and they bowed down and worshiped Him. Then they opened their treasures and presented Him with gifts of gold and of incense and of myrrh."
Matthew 2:11 (NIV)

God gave us His Best Gift, Jesus.
We honor and worship Him when we give Him gifts.

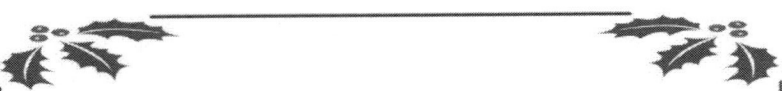

Place the camel, the star and the wiseman at the manger. Repeat the "cue" words for the stable, Mary, Joseph, the angel, the star, the manger, the shepherd (shout!), the camel, the wiseman, the lamb, and Baby Jesus.

HONOR HIM WITH GIFTS

Now it's time for you to give a gift to Jesus.
On a small piece of paper, write your gift to Jesus.
Roll it up and place it next to the manger.

Share your gifts with family and friends with joy
because God has given us
THE BEST PRESENT OF ALL!

MERRY CHRISTMAS!

Grandma has many Bible lessons (in English and Chinese) for families, small groups, and the church.

You will find them at:

www.mygrandmatime.com

Just type "BIBLE FUN" in the search bar.

Also from Grandma:
We're Going to Grandma's House
Fish Friends
Hickory Dickory Dock
Penny Henrow
Chirp
Clyde
Learn to Read with Grandma/Let's Read Together
Draw with Grandma
Sing with Grandma
AND MUCH MORE!

Please visit Grandma at
www.mygrandmatime.com

...doing simple things together!

Made in the USA
Columbia, SC
27 November 2023